Presented to:

_____

By:

_____

Date:

_____

Faith Kids™ is an imprint of
Cook Communications Ministries, Colorado Springs, CO 80918
Cook Communications, Paris, Ontario
Kingsway Communications, Eastbourne, England

THE BABE IN THE MANGER
Text copyright © 2001 by Susan Ankeny
Illustrations copyright © 2001 by Susan Morris

Edited by Phyllis Williams
Designed by Dana Sherrer of iDesignEtc.

First printing, 2001
Printed in Singapore
05 04 30 02 01   5 4 3 2 1

CIP applied for
ISBN 0-7814-3644-3

The Babe in the Manger

Written by Susan Ankeny
Illustrated by Susan Morris

Faith
KiDs®

Equipping Kids for Life
A Faith Parenting Guide is found on page 32.

In loving memory of my father
and in honor of my mother,
who first taught me to love Jesus
and enjoy words.

...The time came for the baby to be born,
and Mary gave birth to her first-born, a son.
She wrapped him in cloths and placed him in a manger,
because there was no room for them in the inn.

Luke 2: 7-9 (NIV)

This is the babe in the manger.

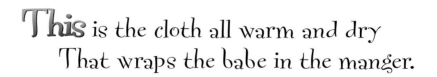

This is the cloth all warm and dry
That wraps the babe in the manger.

This is the mother lovingly nigh who hums
   a silvery lullaby
And smoothes the cloth all warm and dry
   That wraps the babe in the manger.

This is the father giving a sigh
Watching the mother lovingly nigh who hums
    a silvery lullaby
And smoothes the cloth all warm and dry
    That wraps the babe in the manger.

These are the lambs that quietly lie
Close to the father giving a sigh
Watching the mother lovingly nigh who hums
a silvery lullaby
And smoothes the cloth all warm and dry
That wraps the babe in the manger.

This is the donkey gentle and shy
That nuzzles the lambs that quietly lie
Close to the father giving a sigh
Watching the mother lovingly nigh who hums
a silvery lullaby
And smoothes the cloth all warm and dry
That wraps the babe in the manger.

These are the doves in the stable bay
That coo at the donkey gentle and shy
That nuzzles the lambs that quietly lie
Close to the father giving a sigh
Watching the mother lovingly nigh who hums
a silvery lullaby

And smoothes the cloth all warm and dry
That wraps the babe in the manger.

This is the cow that munches hay
Beneath the doves in the stable bay
That coo at the donkey gentle and shy
That nuzzles the lambs that quietly lie
Close to the father giving a sigh

Watching the mother lovingly nigh who hums
a silvery lullaby
And smoothes the cloth all warm and dry
That wraps the babe in the manger.

This is the stable cozy and still
    Where stands the cow that munches hay
Beneath the doves in the stable bay
    That coo at the donkey gentle and shy
    That nuzzles the lambs that quietly lie
    Close to the father giving a sigh
Watching the mother lovingly nigh who hums
    a silvery lullaby
And smoothes the cloth all warm and dry
    That wraps the babe in the manger.

Here are the shepherds from up on the hill
  To visit the stable cozy and still
Where stands the cow that munches hay
Beneath the doves in the stable bay
  That coo at the donkey gentle and shy
  That nuzzles the lambs that quietly lie
  Close to the father giving a sigh
Watching the mother lovingly nigh who hums
  a silvery lullaby
And smoothes the cloth all warm and dry
  That wraps the babe in the manger.

Angels sing with all their might
　　Prompting the shepherds from up on the hill
　　To visit the stable cozy and still
Where stands the cow that munches hay
Beneath the doves in the stable bay
　　That coo at the donkey gentle and shy
　　That nuzzles the lambs that quietly lie
　　Close to the father giving a sigh

Watching the mother lovingly nigh who hums
        a silvery lullaby
And smoothes the cloth all warm and dry
    That wraps the babe in the manger.

This is the star that dazzles the night
  While angels sing with all their might
  Prompting the shepherds from up on the hill
  To visit the stable cozy and still
Where stands the cow that munches hay
Beneath the doves in the stable bay
  That coo at the donkey gentle and shy
  That nuzzles the lambs that quietly lie
  Close to the father giving a sigh
Watching the mother lovingly nigh who hums
  a silvery lullaby
And smoothes the cloth all warm and dry
  That wraps the babe in the manger.

The Angel said . . .
"Do not be afraid. I bring you good news
of great joy that will be for all the people.
Today in the town of David a Savior has
been born to you; he is Christ the Lord.
This will be a sign to you: You will find a baby
wrapped in cloths and lying in a manger."

Luke 2:10-12 (NIV)

The Babe in the Manger

Age: 4-7

My child's need: To know that Jesus came to earth as a baby.

Biblical value: Faith

LEARNING STYLES

Sight: Your children will be delighted with the poetic style of this story. As you read it, your child will begin to memorize the lines and will be able to repeat it back to you. Take turns reading the story in the days prior to Christmas. Your child may want to share the story with friends and relatives who visit your home during the holidays.

Sound: The sounds of the Christmas season leave long-lasting memories in a child's heart. After you have read this story, sing "Away in a Manger" or "Silent Night." Talk about the meaning of these songs, and emphasize the importance of Christ's coming to save people from their sin.

Touch: If you have a nativity scene, use it as a visual aid when reading this story to your child. Have him or her put the manger on a table, and then add pieces as you read the story. When the story is finished, talk to your child about why Jesus came to earth and what His coming means to us. Pray, thanking God for the gift of His Son, Jesus.